# SPARTANAT RED BOOK

# 2

SPARTANAT

www.spartanat.com

ISBN: 978-3-903526-06-8

# BREVIARY OF TACTICS

HANS FRICK

# TABLE OF CONTENTS

# 1 INTRO-DUCTION

# THE COMPACT ART OF WAR

## BY KAJ-GUNNAR SIEVERT

Since the Russian army attacked Ukraine on February 24th, 2022, many armed forces' specialists in the fields of analysis, strategy, theory, and practice have been closely monitoring the course of hostilities. They are trying to draw conclusions from the first war on the European continent in the 21st century, even before the outcome is certain. On the one hand, their own current military guidelines on security policy are to be reviewed and, if necessary, adapted; on the other, possible inferences are to be drawn for the further development of their own armed forces.

All this with the aim of ensuring that their own armed forces will be able to survive and win possible conflicts and wars in the future.

Even though evaluation and knowledge gain will be far from complete by the time this new edition of Hans Frick's "Brevier der Taktik" is printed, profound and fundamental lessons from the Ukraine War are already apparent today, some of which require immediate action. These include, among others:

- **The enormously high consumption of ammunition since the start of the fighting requires a correspondingly large stockpile.**

---

- **The massive use of simple kamikaze drones calls for inexpensive and widely available means of defense and new approaches to combating such systems.**

---

- **A well-organized surface-to-air defense can limit and prevent the use of manned aircraft and cruise missiles.**

---

- **The use of artificial intelligence (AI) on the battlefield will increase.**

---

- **OSINT (Open Source Intelligence) findings are an important piece of the puzzle for drawing conclusions about the enemy. Information from freely accessible sources is widely used and becoming increasingly significant for military operations.**

---

However, it is not a new insight that the will to fight depends on various factors. These include the conviction of having the right on one's side, the value of military training, and confidence in one's own leadership and ability. Military training, in particular, is one of the decisive factors in the will to fight. It is and remains the basis of discipline and can compensate for other factors, such as quantitative superiority or better equipment on the opponent's side.

# KEEP IT SIMPLE

## PRINCIPLES OF WARFARE

It is precisely such core statements that can be found in the "Breviary of Tactics," written by Hans Frick in 1943, in the fourth year of World War II in Europe. The intention of the then-Major General of the Swiss Armed Forces was to record and lay down basic statements about warfare in simple sentences. In other words, principles to explain and convey the core of tactics in a "universally valid and simple" way for readers of all ranks.

The art of war has changed and developed considerably since this book's first edition. However, warfare is and remains ultimately crude and radical, and, as Frick goes on to write, its aims are "victory and destruction of the enemy." Despite these changes, this publication contains basic principles that are still valid today—80 years after its publication.

In his almost 100-page book, Hans Frick describes in 13 chapters concisely formulated core statements on tactics. Military leaders and soldiers who take the straightforward statements set out in more than 280 sections into account in their military decision-making, leadership, and deployment are already acting correctly in many cases. This is because well-thought-out tactics in decision-making help to maximize the effectiveness and efficiency of troops and soldiers while minimizing the risk of casualties. It enables the leader to make optimum use of his forces to achieve his objectives. This is regardless of the initial situation, whether it is a defensive or offensive operation. At best, effective tactics can also help boost the morale of the troops.

In the modern Swiss Armed Forces, tactics are covered in the "Tactical Leadership 17" (TF 17) regulations; the number refers to the year of introduction, i.e., 2017. These regulations have been regularly revised and adapted in the past. The current version of the regulations on tactical command and control comprises around 275 pages, with ten chapters and just as many appendices.

TF 17 is the regulation for tactical command and is subordinate to the regulations of the next higher two levels, "Operational Leadership 17" (OF 17) and "Military Strategic Leadership 17" (MF 17).

TF 17 is one of the three most important command regulations of the Swiss Armed Forces. These regulations contain the principles, set the standards, and serve as guidelines for action across all three levels of command. What they have in common is that they guarantee the commander's freedom of action, restricting it only to the extent necessary for coordination.

TF 17 contains the principles for leadership at a tactical level and is aimed at officers and other cadres. It is therefore not a set of regulations for soldiers. This is where TF 17 differs from the "Breviary of Tactics." In the case of TF 17, the leader determines and is responsible for his actions.

While Hans Frick's book is not intended to be a set of regulations and is short and concise in its style, it is not surprising that TF 17 is more detailed and comprehensive in terms of both content and scope.

What the "Breviary of Tactics" and TF 17 have in common is that they describe principles and procedures that serve as points of reference for the reader and as guidelines for tactical action.

With his work, Hans Frick, a conservative and patriotic officer, laid the foundations that would have been of valuable service to the Swiss Armed Forces in the event of defensive action during World War II. His booklet is also an expression of his attitude of unconditional resistance in the event of an attack by the Wehrmacht.

The breviary aroused the interest of his former enemies both during the war and even more so after the war.

During the war, Hans Frick's skills as a tactician were recorded by the German Army High Command (OKH).

In a document dated September 1942, the General Staff of the Army, Detachment Foreign Armies West, mentions a "Small Orientation Booklet Switzerland" for the first time.

The German document, classified as a "Secret Command Document," describes Switzerland and its army in several chapters from the perspective of the Wehrmacht. The surprisingly neutral booklet was added in December 1944. It seems that the "Breviary of Tactics" by Major General Hans Frick, first published in 1943, also found its way to Berlin. In the list of attachments, he is listed alongside numerous other officers in Appendix 8 among the senior leaders of the Swiss Armed Forces. The comments on him include the following: "Proficient general staff officer, good instructor, especially for tactics [!], but probably not a troop leader [...]."

After the war, the book was translated into French and Spanish. American officers studied the book later as well, but it took until now for an English translation.

# CLEAR THOUGHTS AND BASIC RULES

Even if armed conflicts and wars have evolved in their nature and form up to the present day due to the development of weapons, tactics remain an important piece of the decision-making process of military leadership.

The merit of the work lies in the fact that it became a classic for military tactics thanks to its straightforward train of thought and presented the unchanging principles of war very clearly.

The "Breviary of Tactics" is thus to be seen in the same line of thought as the 19 "Standing Orders" maxims written by Lieutenant Colonel Robert Rogers in 1759. Rogers, who led his British men into an unconventional war against the French in North America, wrote simple principles for combat. Those principles still form the core of the U.S. Army Rangers' "handbook" today.

Compared to Robert Rogers, Hans Frick's "Breviary of Tactics" is unfortunately not reflected in the basic documents of the Swiss Armed Forces in the same way. The work certainly deserves it.

## KAJ-GUNNAR SIEVERT

*born 1965, commanded the Swiss Armed Forces' Parachute Reconnaissance Company, and is now Head of Communications at armasuisse.*

*Author of numerous publications on military history, especially regarding special forces in Switzerland and abroad, including:*

*"Honor – Modestias – Unitas. Das Kommando Spezialkräfte der Schweizer Armee" (2023, on Swiss special forces), "Überall und jederzeit – US Special Forces im Einsatz" (2012, on U.S. special forces), "Die 17er. Die Fallschirmaufklärer der Schweizer Armee" (2011, on the Swiss Parachute Reconnaissance Company).*

# BREVIARY OF TACTICS

HANS FRICK

# PREFACE

This book is the result of many years of teaching and leading courses for the General Staff and higher troop command, as well as of personal command experience. The views the author developed based on the history of war have been generally confirmed during the Second World War. In particular, it has been shown that the views widely held after the First World War, according to which modern weaponry was supposed to have invalidated the centuries-old laws of war and required completely new principles, are incorrect. These views set their supporters up for nothing but defeats. They arose from a way of looking at the external course of events exclusively, overlooking the deeper causes. Yet, they are also an expression of the characteristic bourgeois need for security that can be traced through the 19th century and the first following decades in all areas of life, at least as long as its material basis was preserved.

Division Headquarters, May 1943, in the fourth year of the Second World War

**The author**

# INTRODUCTION

Tactics books are usually thick and quickly become outdated. In addition to basic explanations, they contain a lot of procedural information. These procedures are highly time-dependent and depend on the current state of weapons and equipment technology. In peacetime, they represent the totality of conclusions drawn from the experiences of the last major war, mostly evaluated from only one side, or are the result of speculative considerations about the effect and possible uses of new weapons and equipment or significant improvements to such.

Procedures change rapidly during war. They are the result of experience from the last battles or arise from the desire to surprise the enemy with new methods and thus prevail. The tactical and technical instructions issued by army commands over the course of a long war are evidence of this development.

This publication is not intended to be a textbook on tactics. Everything that is somehow related to our times and the current state of military technology has been excluded. Nevertheless, it goes without saying that the weapons and means of warfare available today have been taken into account to a large extent.

The breviary will confine itself to providing tactical principles that retain a timeless character and will ultimately be decisive for every battle.

# I. GENERAL REMARKS

**1.** "War is the continuation of politics by other means" (Clausewitz). A war's political aim can be positive, radical, and aimed at changing the existing political state, or it can be negative, conservative, and aimed at preserving it.

**2.** Regardless of the nature of the war's aim, the combat objective must always be positive, aimed at victory, the destruction of the enemy. Simply wanting to fend off the enemy's blows leads to defeat. Fighting without aiming for victory must sometimes be done only for secondary tasks and only with partial forces.

**3.** War and battle are governed by eternal, unchangeable laws. New weapons and new means, whatever they may be, only change their external forms, never their essence.

**4.** The laws of combat are simple. In the reality of war, however, it is often law against law. A weak character fails because of the confusing abundance of conflicting demands. Only those who combine an iron character with clear, cool thinking are able to fully recognize which demands of the laws of war have priority in a given case, and whether and to what extent compromises between them are necessary.

**5.** Human weakness always searches for battle procedures—infallible recipes for victory—to which it would like to cling under the pressure of danger and responsibility. But just like life in general, the struggle cannot be forced into rigid forms. No procedure of any kind can guarantee success. Those who commit themselves to such a system lose their inner freedom and thus one of the most important prerequisites for victory.

Training the troops makes it necessary to practice certain forms of combat. However, the supreme command must always remain aware that this training only applies to an assumed "regular case" and that the irregular case of a particular situation may require completely different measures. Only those who are able to master these forms confidently as well as neglect them just as confidently can compel victory onto their side; those who allow themselves to be dominated by them are doomed.

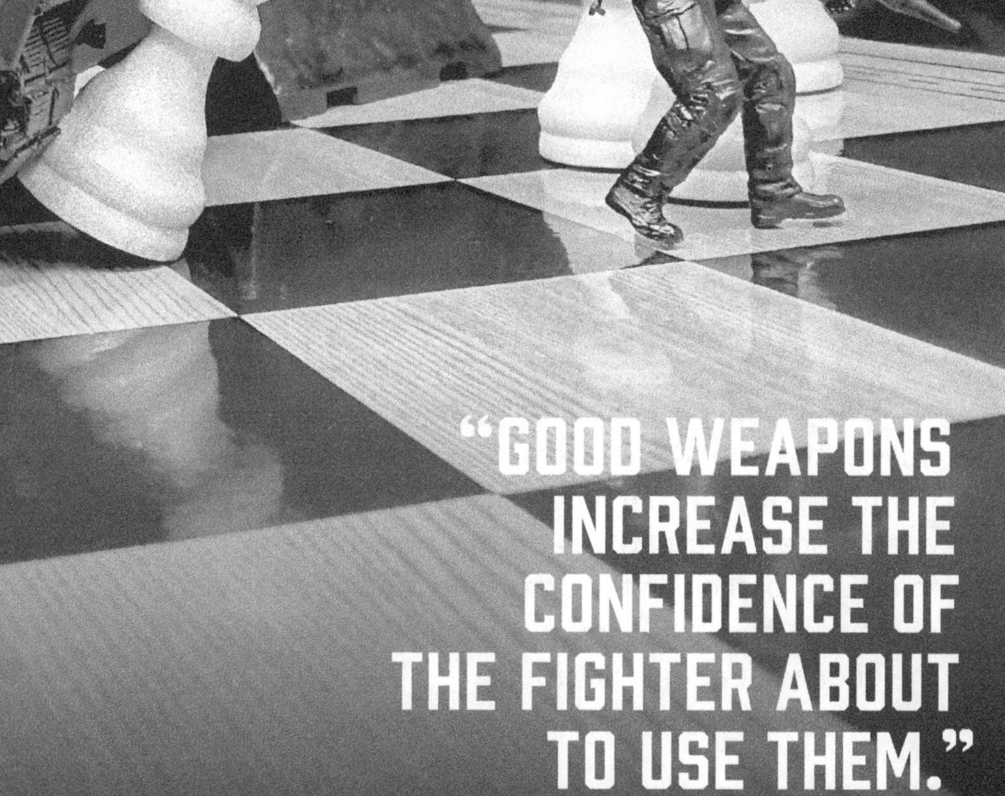

"GOOD WEAPONS INCREASE THE CONFIDENCE OF THE FIGHTER ABOUT TO USE THEM."

Means of Combat, II.8

# II. MEANS OF COMBAT

**1.** The aim of combat is victory, the destruction of the opponent. Destruction is physical only in a limited sense; it rather means the destruction of the enemy's resistance. The means of combat serve this goal.

**2.** The means of combat are:

- — man,
- — weapons,
- — fortifications,
- — passive means of defense.

**3.** **Man** is and remains the noblest means of war. He operates the weapons and other military gear; where he fails, the best war machines are of no use. Even without weapons, he can continue to fight thanks to his natural physical strength and intelligence.

**4.** Every battle is directed against people, i.e., against the enemy's soldiers. It is neither possible nor necessary to completely incapacitate them on a large scale; the battle is decided when their will to resist is broken. In the end, every battle is a psychological one; it is directed against the souls of the enemy's leaders and troops.

**5.** In battle, the will to combat of leaders and troops is decisive first and foremost; superior numbers, quantity and quality of matériel, and mere skill are of secondary importance.

**6.** The will to combat depends on the martial disposition of the people, on the conviction to be righteous, on military training, on confidence in the leadership and in their own ability, and on the physical condition of the soldier.

**7.** Of all the factors of the will to combat, martial education is the most important; it replaces what the modern man of culture lacks in martial disposition, and it creates the discipline without which no success in battle is possible in the long run. It largely makes up for the unfavorable effects of other factors.

**8.** Good **weapons** increase the confidence of the fighter about to use them.

**9.** A bad weapon in the hands of a brave soldier is better than the most perfect weapon in the hands of a coward.

**10.** There are no new weapons against which there are no countermeasures and passive means of protection found in a short time.

**11.** The numbers and kinds of weapons are manifold; in a well-organized army, they are geared to each other like the stops of an organ.

**12.** Good leadership deploys each weapon in such a way that its particular merit is fully effective. Every leader must know the performance and effect of the weapons at his disposal, as well as the limitations and special conditions to which their use is subject.

**13.** Where the most suitable weapon for a task is not available, a less suitable weapon will be used. At close range, almost any weapon can be used with some degree of success.

**14.** Those who have imperfect and few weapons seek close combat. In close combat, even primitive weapons have their significance; the soldiers' manhood is almost the sole deciding factor here.

**15.** Ranged weapons are command-level weapons; close combat weapons are largely those of the individual fighter. Handguns, including automatic weapons, can, to a limited extent, be used for both purposes.

**16.** Ranged weapons serve to prepare the decision; their effect creates the mental state in the opponent that enables one's own troops to enter the final battle with inner superiority.

**17.** Close combat weapons serve to destroy the opponent in the decisive battle; if they are designed as slashing or thrusting weapons, they represent a direct reinforcement of the fighter's physical strength.

**18.** The physical effect of ranged weapons is low in relation to the effort required; accuracy decreases with increasing distance. The effect is reduced even further by the enemy breaking up its formation and all measures that make it more difficult to identify targets.

**19.** Each ranged weapon has its own optimal engagement distance that promises the best physical effect; this must always be sought. Exclusive use of long ranges and long-distance observation shooting must remain the exception.

**20.** The effectiveness of ranged weapons depends on observation; unobserved fire is usually worthless. If ranged weapons are not used to destroy fixed targets, it must be possible to observe not only the position of hits but also the positions of hostile troops in the field of fire; otherwise, the fire is tactically worthless, or it harms one's own troops.

**21.** The moral effect of fire depends on the physical effect; ineffective fire raises the enemy's will to fight instead of weakening it. Further contributing to the moral effect are the bang of the shot as well as the explosion of the grenade and other strong noises caused by the weapon, the obstruction of the enemy's sight by smoke, and the enemy's feeling of lacking effective countermeasures at the moment.

**22.** The moral effect of ranged weapons is multiplied by the temporal and spatial concentration of fire, as well as by their surprising use.

**23.** In principle, all fire that does not serve to destroy material or cover is aimed at destroying the enemy. Where this cannot be achieved with the available means, it may be sufficient in many cases to force the enemy into cover and hamper the use of his weapons. Fire of this kind has no lasting effect; once it has ended, the enemy will soon resume his activities. Merely disrupting the enemy is usually of little value; it is generally only worthwhile if the situation demands it, in order to gain time.

**24.** Fire without a specific tactical purpose is worthless. Anyone who fires or lets others fire without wanting to solve a task within the scope of combat action proves that he lacks a clear idea of combat or that he wants to numb his inner restlessness with the fire.

At any given moment, the fire must either facilitate a certain activity of one's own troops or smash or delay the enemy in decisive phases of the battle.

Only where the enemy offers such a favorable target that it can be destroyed by surprise fire may fire be used outside the immediate scope of the battle.

**25.** Ranged weapons include machine guns and, in a limited sense, rifles, as well as heavy infantry weapons, artillery, rocket weapons, and aircraft.

**26.** The trajectories of long-range firearms are decisive for their use.

A flat trajectory corresponds to a short duration of flight and high penetrating power of the projectiles, good effect against upright cover, and ineffectiveness against targets covered by terrain or buried deep in the ground; weapons of this type are best used against moving targets. The high mobility of the target requires a very short duration of flight for the projectile.

Parabolic trajectories correspond to long flight times and lower penetration power of the projectiles, great effect against shallow cover and targets covered by such or by the terrain; weapons of this type are best used against stationary targets.

**27.** Most long-range firearms can be aimed directly or indirectly; indirect aiming is the rule for artillery. Indirect aiming delays the readiness to fire and impedes the effect against fast-moving enemies; where the situation is urgent or against enemies close nearby, no weapon suitable for flat trajectory firing must shy away from direct aiming.

**28.** The various weapons are usually available in lighter and heavier models, depending on the surface, range, or caliber. Lighter weapons are more maneuverable and easier to cover, but less effective. They are intended for front-line fighting and against more vulnerable targets.

Heavier weapons typically take longer to deploy; they tend to be positioned further behind in battle and are normally intended for use against more resistant targets.

**29.** The well-directed fire of infantry weapons is the best means of obliterating enemy combatants; however, its moral effect frequently lasts no longer than the physical effect and does not extend much spatially.

**30.** The material effect of artillery against moving or well-covered targets is not significant in relation to the ammunition expenditure; its moral effect, on the other hand, is long-lasting and spatially extensive.

Apart from aerial bombs, heavy-caliber artillery is the only effective weapon for destroying stationary targets with a certain resistance.

**31.** The deployment of artillery and the triggering of its fire requires time-consuming preparations. Only a foresighted command ordering them according to the development of the situation can count on the timely engagement of the artillery.

**32.** From their bases, the air forces are operational across a much wider area than artillery and are largely unhampered by terrain conditions that hinder earth observation. Their appearance easily creates a feeling of defenselessness in the enemy. Their moral effect is stronger than that of artillery, while their physical effect is far more dependent on external circumstances, above all on the possibility of clearly recognizing targets from the air and distinguishing friend from foe.

**33.** Self-propelled weapons (self-propelled artillery vehicles, assault guns, and armored cars) combine great firepower with high mobility and usually also with great resistance to enemy fire (armor protection). They can provide powerful fire support at short range in an attack and quickly break through or even shatter the front of a weak, disorganized, or demoralized enemy.

Their appearance in the enemy's rear causes severe disruption or even panic. Their mobility allows for a surprising shift of the center of gravity during an attack.

Their use is highly dependent on terrain and surface conditions. They offer large targets, and their movement mechanism is sensitive.

**34.** The way in which weapons are transported influences their use. Motorized transport gives the leader greater maneuverability and allows the combat equipment to be brought to the decisive position quickly. Troop formations that are equipped with motorized vehicles that allow direct transport onto the battlefield are particularly suitable for preempting the enemy, gaining important advantages, operating against the flanks and rear, and exploiting successes.

**35.** Chemical weapons heavily rely on surprise; where this is lacking, the enemy can easily reduce or even eliminate their effect through countermeasures. Depending on the circumstances, they can endanger or at least hinder your own troops. They are of little use if the enemy must be expected to respond in kind.

**36.** Melee weapons are versatile and can easily be made from makeshift gear. Their use depends on the specific task at hand. Unless this imposes constraints, each fighter chooses the melee weapon that suits his personal disposition best.

**37.** <u>**Fortifications**</u> can be valuable bases or dangerous constraints of combat.

**38.** The value of fortifications lies in the constant readiness of weapons, ammunition, and everything the crew needs to fight and survive, in the preparations made long in advance for the most effective use of weapons, in protection against enemy fire and against assaults from any side. Fortifications are able to hold, even if they are bypassed and attacked from all sides.

**39.** The disadvantage of fortifications lies in the inflexibility of their range of action and in the fact that they become known to the enemy sooner or later and will therefore offer little or no surprise.

**40.** There are no impregnable fortifications, and there never will be.

**41.** Any fortification is worth only what the men defending it are worth. The weapons of a fortification, the resistance of its walls, its roofing, and its armor, and the resistance of its front, flank, and gorge are dead capital; only the soldierly will to combat of the commander and the garrison brings the fortification to life and makes it bear rich fruit.

**42.** Fortifications can be used

— to fight to gain time, to secure the deployment of troops in the rear,
— as a shoulder point or flank support for mobile troops,
— as a means of channeling the enemy's attack.

**43.** Advanced fortifications before the frontline that are to cover formations deployed behind them and are left to themselves will be surrounded by the enemy and succumb to him sooner or later; apart from their garrison's willingness to fight, their resilience depends on their size, the strength of their defenses, and the available reserves of ammunition and provisions. This use of fortifications is an exception and is eligible only when the result obtained justifies the certain loss of valuable combatants and weapons.

**44.** Fortifications are most effective in direct synergy with mobile troops. They then form either the most important pillars of a defensive front or the support for offensive operations.

They are most successful when they hold the enemy and allow your own troops to attack him from the flank or rear.

**45.** Fortifications direct the enemy's movements in certain directions even after their chain has been broken, and some of them may have fallen. The leader can use this to await the enemy behind a line of fortifications and destroy the isolated attacking columns that are already weakened or hindered by the fortifications' weapons in a surprise counterattack.

**46.** When used as passive barriers, unrelated to the fighting of the mobile troops, fortifications are of little value and quickly succumb to enemy attack. This use does not justify the loss of valuable fighters, weapons, and ammunition, nor the high cost of their construction.

**47.** He who hides in fortifications for the sole purpose of evading mobile combat and man-to-man fighting prepares his defeat; the fortification becomes the tomb of his will to combat instead of an aid to victory.

**48.** He who employs mobile troops, which would be needed more urgently elsewhere, for the protection of a fortification without the intention of fighting the decisive battle there transforms this valuable means of fighting into a serious danger.

**49.** **Passive means of defense** reduce the effectiveness of the enemy's weapons or make his movements more difficult.

**50.** The effect of the enemy's weapons is impaired by

- — breaking up combat formations and means of combat,
- — impairing the enemy's sight by artificial means,
- — creating artificial covers.

**51.** Breaking up combat formations and means of combat scatters the enemy's fire and considerably reduces its physical effect. However, it complicates command and control and the coherent deployment of forces. It prolongs the time required to establish combat readiness. It may only be used to the extent that it is required by the expected enemy weapons effect.

**52.** Impairing the enemy's sight makes his fire impossible, or at least imprecise. In addition to the use of terrain, this is achieved by using disguises against ground visibility, camouflage against visibility from above, and, in many cases, smoke screens. Impairing the enemy's sight is the most important passive means of defense; it compensates for the superiority of the enemy's means of combat and makes surprises and ambushes possible.

**53.** Artificial covers (field fortifications) reduce the vulnerability of troops and weapons within them; they must be created wherever a formation is taking up a position in battle or is temporarily forced to stay put. The construction of field fortifications within a formation, the utilization of which is intended for a certain duration, requires detailed prior reconnaissance, careful planning, and lots of time and manpower for the execution.

Anyone constructing field fortifications must be aware of what can be completed in the time available. It is better to have a few finished fortifications at critical points than many half-finished ones, which often reveal more to the enemy than they are of use to your own troops. Every field fortification planned for long-term use must leave open the possibility of later additions and expansions during initial planning already.

When planning field fortifications, the decisive factor must be the desire to harm the enemy, not to evade the enemy's actions.

Field fortifications that make it much easier for the enemy to recognize our own measures usually do more harm than good.

**54.** In addition to certain terrain features, the enemy's movements are made more difficult by artificial obstacles. These include

- — infantry obstacles,
- — obstacles against all-terrain vehicles,
- — mine barriers,
- — the demolition of communications and bridges.

**55.** The purpose of impeding the enemy's movements with obstacles is to give the command the necessary time to deploy its own forces, or to hold the enemy within its own weapons' range of fire and expose him to their maximum effect. Obstacles must also be an expression of the will to win and not of fear; otherwise, they are dangerous.

**56.** In battle, no obstacle can replace one's own troops; it merely creates better conditions for their deployment.

**57.** There is no artificial obstacle that the enemy cannot destroy. Admittedly, this is never possible within a reasonable time in the case of a wide obstacle. Even a partially destroyed obstacle impedes the enemy's movements and directs them in a certain direction towards the breaches made.

**58.** The value of an obstacle depends on its depth, on the resilience of the material used, on the possibility of being guarded by friendly troops or covered by friendly fire, and on its obfuscation against hostile long-range and air reconnaissance. An obstacle that the enemy only recognizes at close range is particularly effective.

**59.** Obstacle construction takes a lot of time, material, and manpower and requires foresighted planning. Only in confined areas are obstacles quickly constructed and particularly effective.

**60.** Where time and material are not sufficient to build an obstacle that brings the enemy to a complete standstill, an obstacle that merely slows down the enemy's movements and thus allows a longer-lasting weapons effect is still of value.

**61.** The creation of obstacles far beyond one's own frontline or the main combat forces is generally limited to communications blockades in places where bypassing them is impossible or possible only with difficulty and considerable loss of time. The explicit purpose of such obstacles is to gain time. If their removal is time-consuming or dangerous, they need not necessarily be covered by friendly forces. The use of weak detachments for delaying actions at such objects is very often not worthwhile; only if the terrain conditions are particularly favorable for the defender or the situation is urgent does the increased gain in time outweigh the probable loss of the detachments deployed for this purpose.

The effect of such obstacles, especially demolitions, is greatly increased if they are placed one after another in large numbers.

**62.** Obstacles in the forward area must be covered by fire. Where visibility conditions do not permit this, especially in the forest or at night, they can be exploited in such a way that the enemy forcing his way through a breach or gap is attacked and thrown back at the moment of breakthrough. This requires constant observation and prepared shock reserves.

**63.** The layout of infantry and tank obstacles depends not only on the possibility of covering them by fire, but also on the cover the terrain offers to the enemy. Where the conditions favor a covered approach, the obstacle is built particularly wide and solid, or several obstacles are placed one behind the other. In confusing terrain, obstacle courses running in different directions and connected like a net can tempt the enemy to veer away from his objective and cause him to lose orientation.

The initial construction of infantry obstacles must take into account the possibility of future reinforcement from the outset.

**64.** Mine barriers hold the middle ground between passive defense and active means of combat. They can be laid relatively quickly; their removal is time-consuming and dangerous. They are only fully effective if the enemy does not recognize them prematurely. Once a mine barrier has done its job, it is also eliminated. This obstacle is better suited for the fight to gain time than for permanent defense on the spot.

**65.** Demolitions require long-lasting preparations that must be arranged in advance if they have not already been made in peacetime. They have a very sustained effect in terms of gaining time if they are placed at large natural obstacles or in rows, one after the other. However, they also act as an obstacle to one's own operations, as long as the communications blocked by them still have to be used by friendly troops. The timing of their triggering is therefore difficult to determine; everything depends on it being chosen correctly.

# III. NATURAL MEANS OF TACTICS

**1.** In addition to the technical means of combat, tactics also makes use of natural means. These are

- — terrain,
- — weather,
- — lighting.

**2.** The battle takes place in open terrain. Winning terrain marks or holding them against an enemy onslaught is a sign of victory. Air combat is merely a pre-stage for ground combat.

**3.** The terrain favors certain military actions or makes them more difficult. It is part of the art of leadership to recognize and exploit these conditions.

**4.** The peculiarities of the terrain that are decisive for combat are

- — altitude conditions,
- — trenches and watercourses,
- — ground cover,
- — ground conditions.

**5.** Flat terrain facilitates the movements of all types of troops. However, it also favors the effect of firearms with a flat trajectory. In flat terrain, even slight depressions are of great value as cover against opponents standing at the same level; conversely, even slight elevations provide a good overview.

**6.** Rising terrain slows down the movements of troops, making it more difficult for them to evade fire through mobility. Steep terrain can become a real obstacle, preventing the movements of certain types of troops.

**7.** There is no impassable terrain. Selected foot troops can get through anything, and there are resources that allow other troops to overcome apparently impassable terrain as well.

**8.** Altitude provides a great overview, thus offering insight into the enemy's movements and a corresponding long-range weapons effect. However, the weapons effect from a summit or high plateau against the enemy's climbing possibilities is usually limited by terrain; on the slopes, there are areas hidden from gun sight that facilitate an attack. If you want to dominate the rises from the heights, you have to expose your weapons or their observation organs to enemy sight on the edges of the heights.

**9.** The tactical value of a height is determined, on the one hand, by the fact that neither other heights nor the terrain cover in its vicinity obstruct the sight and, on the other hand, by the space it provides for the deployment of one's own troops. If these conditions are favorable, one can speak of a commanding height. The possession of commanding heights is often decisive for success in battle.

**10.** A height whose slopes the defender cannot control with fire from the side is easy to climb. The critical point for the attacker begins on the summit or high plateau, where his own fire support stops.

**11.** Bottlenecks channel troop movements. A formation that passes through a bottleneck can only deploy at its exit. This limits its freedom of action. Attacking an enemy passing through a bottleneck or blocking the bottleneck between his individual columns or in his rear is particularly promising.

**12** Mountains slow down all troop movements considerably and restrict them to a few, widely separated roads and paths, between which only the smallest formations can pass. It allows only a limited number of troops to be deployed, depending on the terrain. It makes it difficult to transport heavy weapons, ammunition, and rations. Here, the supply conditions have a decisive effect on military operations.

**13.** In the mountains, moving formations from one section to another is very time-consuming; the maneuverability of the command is therefore greatly reduced or completely eliminated.

**14.** Cuts and watercourses form obstacles to troop movements; bridges and other crossings have a similar effect to bottlenecks.

**15.** Cuts usually have a watercourse, but it is rarely the watercourse itself that forms the obstacle, but rather the steepness and poor accessibility of the slopes. Where they are very pronounced, these obstacles are more effective than wide watercourses. They limit the movement of troop formations of a certain strength and of vehicles to a few good tracks or existing bridges, which are difficult to replace if destroyed.

**16.** The value of a watercourse as an obstacle is determined by its width, the water level, the flow velocity, the condition of the banks, and the possibility of fire striking the surface of the water. In mountain rivers, water level and flow velocity can fluctuate considerably within a few hours.

**17.** A high flow velocity can make it very difficult or impossible to cross a watercourse, even at moderate water levels.

**18.** High, steep banks make it difficult to bring the means of crossing into the water and to board the crossing troops, as well as to moor and disembark on the other side. They form a certain protection against surprise.

**19.** Winding stretches of river are easier covered by fire. Where conditions make it necessary to set up weapons on the banks themselves, these will be quickly recognized and eliminated by the enemy. In such cases, it is usually preferable not to prevent the crossing of the watercourse itself, but to hold and destroy the enemy by fire on the near side or to throw him back into the river by counterattack. The watercourse then serves not as a direct but as an indirect obstacle.

**20.** Lakes, swamps, and artificial impoundments constitute very considerable obstacles that require many resources to cross.

**21.** No watercourse or body of water forms an absolute obstacle; a loose occupation of the bank cannot prevent the enemy from crossing it.

**22.** If one cannot use as many means for the immediate defense of a watercourse as for another section, it is better to fight flexibly against an opponent who is crowded together at crossing points.

**23.** **<u>Ground cover</u>** influences sight and thus the weapons effect; often, it also provides strong cover.

**24.** Houses, groups of houses, and villages offer solid points of resistance that are not completely devalued even by prolonged shelling or bombardment. Even in ruins and the remains of buildings and cellars, a determined defender can hold out for a long time.

In villages, sight is obstructed, coherent command is made more difficult, and immediate support of the troops by long-range weapons and aircraft is impossible.

Densely populated areas are favorable for defense; a rapid breakthrough is difficult for the attacker.

**25.** Forests obstruct ground and air sight and the effect of long-range fire; they make the coherent command of larger formations more difficult. They are suitable staging areas for troops preparing a surprise attack or ambush and favorable starting points for unconventional warfare operations.

Without continuous obstacles, positions in the interior of the forest can hardly be held; bold bravado will bring success even to the weaker combatant.

Dense and extensive orchards have similar effects on sight and weapons effects as forests.

**26.** Ground elevations and, in some cases, ground cover that obstructs sight divide the terrain into marked-out spaces, the terrain units. In terms of width, these form the natural combat areas for individual formations, and in terms of depth, they are the locations for self-contained sub-actions of a battle.

The extent of a terrain unit is determined by the range of sight and effective range of the weapons available to a formation. What appears to the superior leader as one terrain unit is usually divided into several for the lower leader.

**27.** The ground conditions influence the accessibility and the possibility of building fortifications.

The accessibility of stony or rocky ground is hardly dependent on the weather; on the other hand, fortification work there is laborious and time-consuming.

Swampy terrain hinders the movement of vehicles and occasionally even of infantry, especially in wet conditions. Fortification work there is hampered by the groundwater that fills the installations.

Dry farmland and meadows are the most favorable grounds for the activities of all kinds of formations.

**28.** The **weather** largely influences military operations; command must know how to exploit this fact.

**29.** Clear, dry weather favors the movement of all kinds of formations; persistently bad and wet weather hinders the movement of vehicles outside the good roads and impairs air operations. Loose cloud cover facilitates surprise air attacks.

**30.** Frost and snowfall slow down all troop movements; snowstorms hinder sight and work on weapons.

**31.** Fog hinders ground and air sight and makes it difficult to lead and communicate with larger formations in combat.

**32.** Extremely bad weather conditions, such as heavy thunderstorms, storms, downpours, and fog, favor surprise attacks. They are a valuable aid to the weaker party.

**33.** **Lighting** depends on the season, the time of day, and the weather. It influences sight and, thus, the effectiveness of weapons. Command must take these circumstances into account and utilize them, especially for the timing of combat operations.

**34.** Frontal sunlight impedes sight and combat a lot; sunlight from the rear favors it. A bright background (horizon, snow) reveals movements at long range.

**35.** Strong shadows and poor lighting hinder sight and weapons effects; dark night eliminates them or limits them to the closest distance.

**36.** Twilight and night favor surprise attacks; they are valuable aids to the weaker party. Moonlight nullifies these advantages to a great extent.

# IV. LEADERSHIP

**1.** Apart from the soldierly prowess and skill of the troops, leadership is the most important factor in success; it can largely compensate for the unfavorable effects of other factors, such as inferiority in numbers and armament.

**2.** The task of the leader is threefold:
- he gives the troops moral support,
- he makes the decisions,
- he takes the technical precautions to carry them out.

**3.** Providing moral support for the troops is the leader's most essential task. In some situations, it is the decisive one. The iron will of a determined leader and his personal example drive the troops forward towards the enemy and hold those wavering in their positions; in desperate situations, the leader maintains the will to fight to the death.

**4.** The leader's decision lays down the foundations of a battle. It largely determines victory or defeat.

**5.** The higher up a leader is, the more free decisions he has to make. Subordinate leaders are often only left with the technical implementation of their superiors' decisions. But in the unpredictable circumstances of war and in the confusion of battle, every leader can find himself in the position of having to make independent decisions. The most difficult decision is to deviate from the orders of one's superior.

**6.** The leader must usually make his decision in an unclear situation and under the pressure of danger. Clear and cool judgment of the possibilities and an unswerving will to victory allow him to master even difficult and completely unclear situations.

**7.** He who does not primarily think of destroying the enemy and is eager to meet him in battle, who merely wants to parry his blows, is soon lost.

**8.** A bold resolution is better than a cautious one. Bold decisions regularly bring success; those based on fear bring defeat.

**9.** The leader always seeks surprise attacks. They are the best means to success. They have a strong moral effect on the enemy. Whoever surprises the enemy dictates the law of action to him and prevents him from using his means according to plan.

**10.** The leader's decision answers the questions:
— whether to attack, defend, or retreat,
— whether different tasks are to be solved

simultaneously, and if not, in what order they are to be done,

— how the resources are to be distributed if there are several tasks or several opponents,
— where the opponent should be expected in order to stop or attack him,
— where the center of gravity is to be put,
— whether to open fire and when.

**11.** If it is doubtful whether to attack, defend, or retreat, attack is usually the best solution. A bold attack clarifies the situation and gives the leader an initial success against an opponent who is not fully prepared, thus ensuring his freedom of decision.

Someone fighting for a decision may only order a retreat if victory is no longer possible, and remaining with the enemy would lead to the destruction of their own forces. In the case of other combat tasks, such as those that often fall to subunits, retreat may be necessary because the mission has been accomplished or because it even requires evasion. In these cases, it is important to initiate the retreat before the battle has entered the decisive phase.

The decision to sacrifice oneself and one's troops on the spot means admitting that nothing more can be achieved in open combat. It is a last resort and may only be taken when there is no better way of harming the enemy or when the mission demands it.

No real leader surrenders as long as he has ammunition and rations.

**12.** Where there are several opponents or tasks, the leader must limit himself to the most critical one; only a decision directed towards a goal promises success. Only those secondary tasks that can be solved with limited resources can occasionally be carried out at the same time as the main task. If different tasks have to be fulfilled, those that serve to directly damage the enemy take precedence over those that are aimed at one's own safety.

**13.** If the enemy surprises a formation during the execution of any task, the task of defeating him takes precedence over all others. Only where mission and situation permit evading him may one refrain from fighting him for victory.

**14.** If there are several opponents, the urgency of their engagement is determined by

- — their numbers, equipment, and distances,
- — their positions in relation to important terrain objects, to own neighboring formations, and to own lines of communication,
- — the terrain between them and one's own troops, especially the presence of obstacles.

**15.** When the decision has been made as to which enemy will be dealt with first, defense against the others must be carried out with a minimum of means during this first combat action.

**16.** The leader who wants to wait for the enemy to stop him in place or attack him during his advance chooses a terrain that limits the sight and use of the enemy's heavy means of combat, while favoring the use of one's own forces.

**17.** The center of gravity of a combat action is formed by the massive use of ranged weapons and melee combatants. As a rule, it is located where conditions are most favorable for the effect of the long-range weapons and their combined direction. For the purpose of surprise, the leader can also place the center of gravity in a less favorable area.

**18.** The leader will open fire on a target only if the expenditure of ammunition and the exposure of his own firing position are worthwhile. The physical effect that can be achieved under the given circumstances is secondary to the expected tactical success.

**19.** The leader may reserve the order to open fire for entire formations or categories of weapons for himself, in order to surprise the enemy and bring the weapons to bear only at the most effective distance.

Opening fire early slows down the enemy's movements, but allows him to evade; it betrays one's own fire organization. Opening fire late is surprising and—at close range—devastating.

**20.** The foundations of the decision are

- one's own mission,
- available means,
- spatial and temporal conditions,
- terrain and other natural resources,
- intelligence about the enemy.

**21.** The mission must remain the guiding principle from the beginning to the end of combat action. The leader must not allow himself to be distracted by any secondary events or influences from the enemy. Only where circumstances are completely different from those anticipated when the mission was ordered must the leader deviate from the mission on his own.

**22.** The mission follows from the briefing that the leader has received from his superior, from his general intention or battle plan, and from the concrete order that has been given. A clear understanding of the first two points enables the leader to act according to the circumstances and, where necessary, to deviate from the wording of the concrete order given to him in accordance with the mission assigned.

**23.** The absence of a mission is no excuse for inactivity. Those who have no mission act in the interests of the whole. To harm the enemy, to thwart his intentions, is always the decisive aspect.

**24.** The leader may only make decisions that are feasible with the available means, with respect to their spatial distribution and their condition. Anyone who sets tasks that do not comply with this principle is committing self-deception and preparing for defeat. This is particularly true with regard to the relationship between attack or defense fronts and the number of troops and weapons available.

Where the situation forces a task to be solved with insufficient means, forces must be concentrated at decisive points or in decisive directions, leaving gaps. Frittering away resources always leads to failure.

**25.** Space and time play an important role in the leader's decision. Without precise calculation of these factors, even the most energetic leader loses himself in unrealistic fantasies.

Crowding troops into a confined space impairs their maneuverability and exposes them to concentrated fire or attack from the enemy, while placing them in excessively large spaces reduces their impact and resilience.

A careful calculation of the time required for troop movements and the deployment of weapons is essential; it also shows whether time-consuming preparations are permissible or whether a less thorough, but short-term, organization of the battle is required.

In all unexpected situations, rapid action is always better than the laborious preparation of resources.

**26.** The assessment of the terrain is of decisive importance for decision-making. It shows the critical points or spaces for battle and allows one to recognize one's own possibilities and those of one's opponent.

Where conditions permit, the leader inspects the terrain himself. Where this is not or not yet possible, the map is used instead. A careful map assessment provides information on which questions still require clarification through reconnaissance.

**27.** Intelligence about the enemy is an uncertain basis for the leader's decision. Much of it is usually exaggerated or false; even correct information is often outdated by the time it arrives.

Therefore, intelligence only provides an indication of the enemy's capabilities. Anyone who relies on in and concludes with certainty that the enemy will behave in a certain way risks serious disappointment and defeat.

Those who allow themselves to be frightened by alarm and disaster messages demonstrate inner insecurity and succumb to deliberate deception by the enemy. Only combat provides reliable information about the enemy.

**28.** The leader makes his fundamental decision even if there is only a minimum of information about the enemy. The situation falling into place only influences the details of the execution of his plan.

On the other hand, those who make themselves dependent on information about the enemy lose the initiative and leave the law of action to the enemy. They are already half-defeated before the battle even begins.

**29.** The technical measures of leadership include

- arranging divisions and formations,
- defining boundaries between the areas of action of the subunits and the spaces and distances between them,
- assigning positions and observation areas for long-range firearms,
- measures for reconnaissance, communication, and transmission,
- measures to supply the troops with everything necessary for combat and life.

**30.** No technical measures, however perfect, can make up for the lack of a clear decision, an idea of leadership. Where leadership is limited to technique, success depends solely on the efficiency of the troops; the leader has no influence on the outcome of the battle.

**31.** The leader's decision and technical measures of command must seek to achieve maximum synergy among all forces and orderliness in combat operations. The leader must be aware, however, that the numerous frictions of war and the activities of the enemy mean that even his best preparations will only have a partial effect, or perhaps none at all. The fortunes of war often turn in their favor against even the most capable. Those who reckon with this fact from the outset will not be discouraged by it and will master even an unfavorable fate.

**32.** Leadership is not limited to basic decisions and technical measures. Combat is not a spectacle that takes place according to a program. In its course, new decisions and technical measures become necessary constantly. The situation gradually falling into place allows and demands that the tasks of individual formations and weapons be determined more precisely within the framework of the overall plan. It will also be necessary to exploit individual successes and compensate for the effects of setbacks.

**33.** Only those can lead who are close to the frontline and can judge the course of the battle, especially its beginning, from their own perspective.

To do this, the leader chooses a vantage point or goes to the focal point of the battle. However, moving back and forth across the battlefield aimlessly makes leadership difficult and betrays uncertainty. In secondary sections, subordinates check on the situation where necessary.

**34** Decisions and technical measures are reflected in the order. The order conveys the leader's will to his subordinates.

**35.** Through the order, the leader informs his subordinates of his personal view of the enemy situation, informs them of his intention or his battle plan, and assigns each one a role in the overall action. Technical measures of all kinds supplement the order.

**36.** For battle, the presentation of the supreme intention or battle plan is the most important part of the order. It indicates the final objective to be achieved by combat and, in general, the sequence of the most essential actions to achieve it.

**37.** From the leader's orientation on the enemy situation and the presentation of the supreme intention, the subordinate gains an overall picture of the planned action in which he has to play his particular role. Where these are clearly expressed, the order to the subordinate can be kept brief. Whoever prescribes details in his orders where the need for close cooperation does not urgently demand such, betrays uncertainty and mistrust and makes the subordinates incapable of acting freely and responsibly according to the situation.

**38.** The leader plans far ahead, but gives orders only up to the next goal. Anyone who gives specific instructions beyond that is punished by events and must give counter-orders. Counter-orders cause misunderstandings, disorder, and shake the confidence of subordinates.

**39.** The commanding of true leaders has a personal character. It exudes power and simplicity.

Whoever gives orders according to learned patterns and fills them with formulaic stuff demonstrates a lack of intellectual independence and of the ability to lead.

**40.** Each military action is a special case and requires a formulation tailored to it; tactical terminology is not sufficient.

Natural, understandable language is the hallmark of a good order; an erudite, expertly style usually conceals a lack of clear ideas.

**41.** A lot of time can be gained by giving orders skillfully, and a lot more time can be lost by giving orders laboriously. Those who give orders skillfully act quickly.

Staggering orders according to the urgency of the matter and the reception, and placing that which is initially important first, contribute more to the swiftness of an operation than speeding up the pace.

# V. RECONNAISSANCE AND SECURITY

**1.** Reconnaissance and security are the expenses of troop command; whoever spends too much on them weakens the troops for the decisive battle.

**2.** Reconnaissance seeks out the enemy and determines his location, strength, and composition as well as his activities at a given time.

**3.** Ground reconnaissance usually only determines the outline of an area occupied by the enemy, but it can say with certainty whether there is an enemy in a given place at a given time.

Aerial reconnaissance reaches far into the depths of enemy space; however, it does not mean that a space is free of hostile forces if it has not detected anything there.

**4.** Reconnaissance units are sent out in the most critical directions; it is neither possible nor necessary to search every corner of a space that may be occupied by the enemy. Details only become significant in the immediate vicinity of the enemy.

**5.** Reconnaissance units observe; they only fight if this is essential for the fulfillment of their mission or if they have been assigned a security task in addition to reconnaissance.

**6.** Combat by reconnaissance units is usually not worthwhile; where it is no longer possible to slip through enemy barriers without a fight, strong combat units are needed to clarify the situation. Violent reconnaissance is often only an expression of constraint.

**7.** The strength of the reconnaissance units is determined by the number of directions of observation, the number of messengers likely to be sent, and the reporting distance.

Strong reconnaissance units are dispatched if they are to form a support and reporting point for a number of weaker reconnaissance units.

**8.** Each reconnaissance order specifies what the leader wants to know, from where he expects reports, and how long the reconnaissance unit is to remain in a particular area or close to the enemy.

**9.** The reconnaissance units report where they have met the enemy, how he is composed, what he is doing, and when he was observed. It is often important to report that an area is free of hostile forces.

**10.** Each reconnaissance unit reports on the terrain conditions that are essential to the leader, even without an order, unless they can be seen on the map.

**11.** Security units protect against surprise attacks and ambushes. They give the leader time to make decisions and deploy his troops.

**12.** Good reconnaissance and appropriate organization of the troops save cumbersome and energy-consuming security measures.

**13.** Troops at rest or not yet engaged in combat require ample security.

The security of resting troops remains attached to terrain lines that limit the enemy's use of rapid means. It keeps a firm hold of suitable blocking points on the road sections leading up from the enemy, and restricts itself to observation of the intermediate terrain.

During the day, the security of resting troops aims for a wide sight; it works with fire from distance weapons, taking advantage of the long firing ranges.

At night, sight is irrelevant; the decisive factor here is clinging to terrain points that allow freedom from assault, even against attacks from the flank and rear.

**14.** Troops on the march secure themselves in the marching direction by forming a vanguard, which consists of loosely organized detachments and is always sent far ahead. The distance between the main force and the vanguard depends on the terrain; in mountainous terrain, the vanguard must usually be able to reach the summit before the main force begins the ascent.

**15.** In contrast to other security measures, the vanguard has a dependent task; when encountering the enemy, the higher leader decides on its behavior.

**16.** If opposing forces are positioned close to each other in the course of a battle without any actual fighting taking place, or if a battle is interrupted by weather conditions or the night, the frontline constitutes security for the troops resting behind it.

**17.** Flank and rear guards may be necessary for troops at rest, on the march, and in battle. On the march, flank guards may accompany the main force on a secondary route or occupy suitable barriers to the side of the marching route. In all other cases, these securities are typically tied to a specific location.

**18.** Flank and rear guards are not available for the decisive battle. If you want to win, you must not want to secure yourself against all conceivable dangers.

Swift, purposeful action in a decisive direction is the best protection against enemy operations from other directions.

Only where the situation and terrain indicate that a threat to the flanks and rear is highly probable within a dangerous period of time are such security detachments justified.

**19.** Security detachments fight to gain time, either defending or attacking or using a mixture of both methods, depending on the circumstances. Without explicit orders to the contrary, they sacrifice themselves on the spot if necessary.

# VI. GENERAL COURSE OF COMBAT

**1.** Every battle begins with **opening skirmishes**. These are conducted with advance troops and are intended to provide final and definitive reconnaissance, induce the enemy to show his strength, and gain time for the deployment of the main forces.

**2.** Whoever wishes to attack seeks to gain a clear picture of the enemy through the opening skirmishes, to force the mass of the enemy's forces or weapons to intervene, and at the same time to create a favorable starting position for the decisive battle.

Anyone who wants to defend or attack the opponent from a prepared position seeks to wear out the opponent through the opening skirmishes, to deceive him about one's actual intentions, and to cause him to deploy his main forces unwisely.

**3.** The opening skirmishes are followed by the **deployment of the bulk of long-range weapons**. Its purpose is to allow the close combat units to approach to fighting distance or to deny doing the same to the enemy.

In this phase of the battle, it is crucial that the will to combat is maintained despite the losses incurred and despite the grueling mental effect of the noise of fire and of exploding projectiles. Where this is not the case, the decision is already reached at this point, and close combat does not even take place: The attacker comes to a standstill, or the defender runs away.

Only in exceptional cases and only in narrowly localized areas is the physical effect sufficient to make any advance or resistance impossible.

**4.** The long-range firefight, unless it has already decided the outcome of the battle on its own, is followed by **man-to-man combat**. Only here is it finally decided who is the victor. Whoever flees or surrenders shows the opponent that he is submitting to his law.

**5.** The decision is followed by the **exploitation of success**. No success in battle is of lasting importance without being exploited, at least by chasing fire or by pursuit. In the battle itself, both opponents suffer heavy losses, with the victor often suffering the heavier. Only the exploitation of success brings rich rewards. The defeated opponent loses numerous prisoners, has to give up valuable matériel, and his formations fall apart.

**6.** The individual phases of the battle usually merge into one another without any clear demarcation. Only in exceptional cases, such as when night falls, are they clearly separable.

# VII. ARRANGEMENT

**1.** The arrangement of the troops by width and depth makes them ready for action and gives them maneuverability. It provides a geometric expression of the will to lead.

**2.** An extensive depth structure leads to little width structure in the front; it allows the leader to do justice to all possibilities that arise and to adhere to a leading idea while remaining flexible and adaptable in its implementation. It corresponds to an uncertain situation.

**3.** The transition from a strong depth structure to a wide structuring means the increased expenditure of resources for the battle; it indicates that the leader is aware of the enemy and knows in which direction he wants to deploy the bulk of his forces.

Only in the decisive phase of the battle is the depth structure completely abandoned; all resources are then deployed for the final battle.

**4.** Anyone who prematurely abandons the depth structure or greatly reduces it in favor of width deprives himself of the ability to maneuver and risks that subordinate units may encounter the enemy under unfavorable conditions against his will.

**5.** An extensive width structure requires little or no depth structure; this formation is characterized by a strong initial, but impermanent effect.

**6.** Depth structure makes leadership easier; width structure makes it more difficult.

**7.** Formations organized in successive battle lines run the risk of not being able to disperse in time and thus becoming mixed up; this type of arrangement is only suitable when a formation has to move through a confined space.

**8.** Staggered formation to the sides and the rear at the same time provides the best possibilities for maneuvering; it allows the rear lines to be drawn close to the front lines or to be set further away from them, as required, without the need for flanking marches; it makes for the best flank protection.

**9.** The wedge formation is the ideal arrangement for advancing in an unclear situation or when preparing for various possibilities; it allows the front to proceed ruthlessly without fear for the flanks, as well as immediate fronting to any given side. It allows the leader to reserve the formation of a center of gravity until the very end.

**10.** Gaps in the arrangement are determined by the front widths normally allotted to the formations;

they are at least large enough to allow the forward deployment of a unit next to the neighboring one and, in any case, the one straight ahead without a mash-up on the inner wings. The gaps can often be extended a bit beyond this size to achieve slightly concentric movements.

**11.** The normal front width of each formation for attack or defense is determined by experience; open terrain allows larger front widths, while unclear terrain requires smaller front widths. For tasks that do not require sustainability or are only temporary in nature, much larger front widths can be selected than are normally allotted.

**12.** The distances within the arrangement depend on the average firing range of the weapons assigned to the formations, the terrain, visibility, and the combat situation; in larger scenarios, they also depend on the time required to catch up with the forward detachments.

As long as the exact direction of the deployment of a rear unit has not yet been determined, the distances should be approximately 1.5 to 2 times the size of the gaps.

**13.** Troops that are followed by the rear units at too great a distance cannot be supported by them in time; the formation falls apart. This leads to incoherent individual fighting and drop-by-drop deployment of the following units.

**14.** Rear units too close behind lose their maneuverability and easily come under fire aimed at troops ahead, being thus drawn into combat without the leader's intention.

**15.** Terrain and visibility conditions determine how far a rear unit has to stay back in order not to be affected by fire aimed at troops ahead and to be able to move sideways while remaining covered from sight. In any case, it must be possible to deploy next to a forward unit without a pronounced transversal or flanking move. Good visibility requires large distances; poor visibility requires short distances.

**16.** Unclear battle situations require plenty of maneuvering possibilities, i.e., large distances; a clear situation allows the given direction of deployment also of the rear units to be recognizable, which are brought closer accordingly in order to be at hand for the decision.

# VIII. ATTACK

**1.** The attack is the form of combat that alone brings a final decision. Throwing back the enemy and gaining ground are the hallmarks of a successful attack. However, total victory is only achieved if the opponent can be destroyed.

**2.** The attacker chooses the time and location of the attack; it is easy for him to let the surprise work for him.

**3.** The attacker is in constant action and movement, while the defender has to wait. Those who can act are better able to endure the uncertainty of the situation, enemy fire, and losses than those who have to wait.

**4.** The attacker requires superiority. It need not be measured in terms of the number of forces and resources. Superior leadership, fighting morale of the troops, or a more favorable position can make the one who is inferior in numbers capable of mounting an attack. Superiority is by no means necessary on the entire front; it is sufficient to be stronger at the point where the decision is sought.

**5.** The focus of the attack is on one wing or in the center of the enemy's frontline. Where this is not yet clearly visible, it is directed towards a decisive terrain point or against a vital space for the enemy.

**6.** Where the enemy offers an open flank, the attacker seeks the envelopment, the attack against the enemy's flank and rear. A flank or rear attack without simultaneously attacking the front is only successful if the enemy is completely taken by surprise.

Envelopment confuses the enemy's formations, pushes the enemy in an unfavorable direction, cuts through his rear connections, and can even lead to his complete encirclement. Envelopment is particularly successful when it succeeds in pushing the enemy against a strong natural obstacle.

**7.** Envelopment is only effective if it is directed against the depth of the enemy's flank or against the rear; a mere push against the wing ends of the front causes the enemy to turn a defensive flank and is usually unsuccessful.

**8.** Double envelopment is particularly promising, but it requires large forces or otherwise particularly favorable conditions. With small and medium-sized formations, double envelopment can easily lead to a dilution of the main mission and a dispersion of resources. It is better to have resounding success in one place than to get stuck in two.

**9.** An envelopment by airborne troops is impressive, but far less effective against an opponent who keeps his cool than an envelopment by ground troops.

Landing large forces with parachutes and transport aircraft is time-consuming and susceptible to interference. Troops landing close to the front are exposed to counterattacks by the enemy's reserves, against which they can initially only be deployed drop by drop; far from the front, their intervention is hampered by a lack of means of transportation.

**10.** In the mountains, leaning both flanks against difficult terrain usually prevents encirclement; it is then replaced by bypassing.

In easily passable terrain, bypassing is only worthwhile for troops with fast means of transportation; for infantry, it is too time-consuming, can easily be disturbed by the enemy, and leads to the fragmentation of forces.

**11.** Where envelopment or evasion is impossible, the attacker aims for a frontal breakthrough. Breaking through a determined enemy demands time, heavy losses, and a lot of ammunition. Exploiting a successful breakthrough is difficult; it consists of rolling up the front from the breakthrough point. An agile opponent can evade this maneuver, so that the breakthrough merely leads to a frontal pushback of the enemy and thus to no final decision.

**12.** The leader leads the attack by directing the long-range means of combat under his immediate command, and by directing and deploying his rear units or reserves.

**13.** The synergy of fire and movement is of decisive importance for the success of an attack.

**14.** The long-range weapons are deployed close to the frontline in order to be able to support the attack for a long time without changing positions. Changing the positions of important long-range weapons slows down the momentum of the attack.

**15.** The long-range weapons protect the attacking units against threats from the flanks and facilitate their advance by holding down the enemy's frontal fire; they ultimately soften up the enemy for storming.

Command must recognize early when these individual tasks will be necessary and prepare the long-range weapons for them in good time so that the troops do not have to call in fire support first.

**16.** The individual barrages are triggered when the units indicate their readiness to proceed or start moving on their own initiative, or—finally—when a feared threat from the flank is realized by fire or attack. They continue until the zone of greatest danger has been crossed.

A massive barrage is equivalent to the leader ordering an advance.

The assault is preceded by the most intensive fire of all long-range means of combat.

**17.** Rear units are brought up in the direction in which success is expected; they are used for achieving it or exploiting it where it has occurred.

The use of rear units to resume failed attacks at the same location and in the same form usually means a useless sacrifice of valuable forces; it is only considered when there is no other option left.

**18.** At the climax of the battle, the leader uses all means at his disposal to reach a decision. Anyone who still withholds reserves to defend against unexpected events at this time demonstrates a lack of will to win and jeopardizes success.

Success in battle allows for the formation of new reserves without further ado.

**19.** If you want to win without having overwhelming superiority, you must be able to accept and bear setbacks in secondary sections of the battle front. Success at the decisive point makes up for them in any case.

Those who allow themselves to be tempted to deploy forces that should have participated in the decisive blow elsewhere—responding to distress signals from subordinates or to avoid setbacks—let the enemy dictate the rules to them and surrender their success.

**20.** Along with its next object, the leader indicates to each detachment the direction in which to advance further. A designation of lines or points that are not to be crossed without orders impedes the offensive momentum and frequently leads to a complete halt of the advance. This measure may only be taken if the attack has a limited objective rather than a decisive victory.

**21.** Units deployed in the attack advance straight ahead without being stopped by enemy formations positioned to their sides. The protection of their flanks is the responsibility of the superior leader. Only where his preparations are insufficient or not yet effective do they provide flank security themselves with a minimum of troops.

Widening breaches, rolling up the enemy front, and encircling overtaken enemy troops are the responsibilities of rear units.

**22.** Units in contact with the enemy can only advance in a straight line. If the direction has to be changed during the course of battle, rear units must be assembled in the new direction and deployed through the front elements.

**23.** An attack must be conducted differently against an enemy confronted in mutual movement—a meeting engagement—or against an enemy already arranged for combat or even set up for defense.

Particularly favorable conditions are offered by an attack from an assembly area against an enemy on the march or advancing to attack.

**24.** Those who are weaker in numbers and resources avoid the meeting engagement. But any unit on the march, even behind the frontline, can unexpectedly encounter the enemy; in such situations, an attack is the only possible solution.

In their later stages, prepared attacks and even defense take on the character of a meeting engagement. Anyone who has not mastered this form of combat is not a leader.

**25.** The meeting engagement is characterized by great uncertainty about the enemy. Only combat brings clarity about the strength and intentions of the enemy.

**26.** Success in the meeting engagement is largely determined by rapid and superior maneuvering. Those who reach decisive points before the enemy do not have to expend blood and ammunition to conquer them, or to try reaching them in vain.

The leader who anticipates his opponent's actions and is combat-ready faster than the latter forces him into parrying, dictates the law of action to him, and secures success for himself.

**27.** In a meeting engagement, the leader deliberately refrains from cumbersome arrangements and extensive fire organization, which impede the flow of movement.

**28.** For each advance in which there is a certain probability of encountering the enemy, the commander will account to himself at an early stage as to where the decisive points are in each terrain unit where a clash may occur. He thus gains a foundation for his guiding idea and can prepare artillery reconnaissance for the various possibilities in good time.

**29.** The battle is initiated by deploying the vanguard or foremost unit, which clarifies the situation by proceeding briskly, forcing the enemy to show his strength and drawing as much of it as possible onto itself.

To this end, the vanguard advances on a broad front determined by the superior leader within the framework of the battle plan and is supported as quickly as possible by powerful long-range weapons.

It quickly deals with scattered enemy resistance by outflanking it, or it otherwise finds an already deployed enemy.

**30.** Only in exceptional cases, if the enemy has a strong advantage in deploying or if advancing further would lead into particularly unfavorable terrain, can the leader allow the vanguard to cling to the terrain. However, there is always the danger that the enemy will seize control of the action.

**31.** Simultaneously with the deployment of the vanguard, the main force is organized laterally in accordance with the battle idea in such a way that it can either follow the vanguard's approach unit by unit or be deployed to attack. It is drawn forward section by section and remains in the hands of the leader until the vanguard's advance is no longer sufficient and the bulk of the enemy's force appears.

At this point, the main force is deployed to attack uniformly and in unison in the decisive direction, supported by the mass of long-range weapons. The leader decides whether the situation permits a brief assembly for the purpose of greater cohesiveness of attack, or whether the individual units must be deployed from movement.

**32.** An **attack on an enemy deployed or even arranged for defense** requires prior assembly. Here, planning and extensive fire organization are more important than speed.

**33.** The vanguard or the unit closest to the enemy covers the advance into positions; it clings to a suitable terrain line. Behind it, the units of the main force are arranged according to the battle idea in covered assembly areas.

**34.** Tactically decisive for the planning of an attack against a position are

— the spaces into which the attacker has the best sight and thus concentrated fire is possible,
— the spaces that allow a covered approach towards the enemy,
— natural and artificial obstacles in front of the frontline.

**35.** The attack begins—at the earliest—after all preparations have been completed; the time of readiness is usually ordered.

The time of the beginning of the attack is ordered uniformly; this order may be reserved until the last moment.

**36.** It is often necessary to disable the enemy's forward posts or occupy critical points by means of partial operations before the general attack begins.

Where the enemy has established strong cover and obstacles, it is frequently necessary to partially destroy those by heavy fire before the attack begins.

**37.** To penetrate the enemy's front, the combat units require strong concentrated fire at the decisive point.

**38.** **Attacking from an assembly area against an enemy on the march** exploits the advantages of high orderliness, best fire organization, and uniformity of action against an enemy who is not prepared in this respect. Surprise is one of the main conditions for its success.

This type of attack can be realized by the advance of a defender from his position against an enemy deploying, by counterattacking an opponent about to exploit a success, or by an ambush. Such attacks have a limited objective and are not aimed at gaining ground, but at destroying as many enemy units as possible.

**39.** A defender's preemptive attack from his position aims to destroy the enemy's attack preparations before they are completed and to destroy resources. It is particularly effective when the opponent turns his back towards a natural obstacle.

The preconditions are a surprising, usually nocturnal, regrouping of the defender, clear determination of the objective or the line that must not be crossed, and preparations for returning to the position after success, if moving it forward is not an objective.

**40.** A counterattack against an enemy in the process of exploiting his success requires an early movement of the reserves intended for this purpose into the anticipated operational area, normally on the flank of the enemy's advance and covered by the parts of the front still held.

**41.** The ambush is an effective means for the weaker party. A successful ambush has a lasting moral and, typically, a great physical effect. It can only be carried out with complete success in terrain that impedes the enemy's freedom of movement and offers the troops covered and not easily accessible assembly areas. Mountainous and wooded terrain is particularly suitable for this. A bold and, correspondingly, unsecured approach by the enemy creates favorable conditions for ambushing.

**42.** The ambush is primarily carried out with fire. The attack, in a narrower sense, only begins afterward and has the sole purpose of finishing off the enemy, who is already confused and severely weakened by losses. Under certain circumstances, this last phase of the battle can be omitted altogether.

An ambush can only begin with the thrust if it is possible to get within close combat distance from the enemy unseen.

**43.** Prerequisites for the success of an ambush are

- — deployment of the assault units to the side of the enemy's axis of advance and on a height or behind a terrain obstacle that precludes the enemy's rapid access to these weapons,
- — a good overview and large fields of fire,
- — allowing enemy reconnaissance and security detachments to pass and fighting them further away; inconspicuous destruction of all reconnaissance units moving towards the assembly area itself,
- — blocking the enemy's further advance far beyond the ambushing point,
- — protecting the flank against following-up enemy forces; in any case, blocking the axis of advance behind the unit to be attacked.

**44**. In all attacks of this type, determining the time to launch the attack is of the utmost importance, but often very difficult. Especially in the case of an ambush, the leader must keep cool and wait until the enemy presents himself in a form that is susceptible to loss. The ambush is aimed at the enemy's flank and rear; frontal ambushes are only successful in the smallest of proportions.

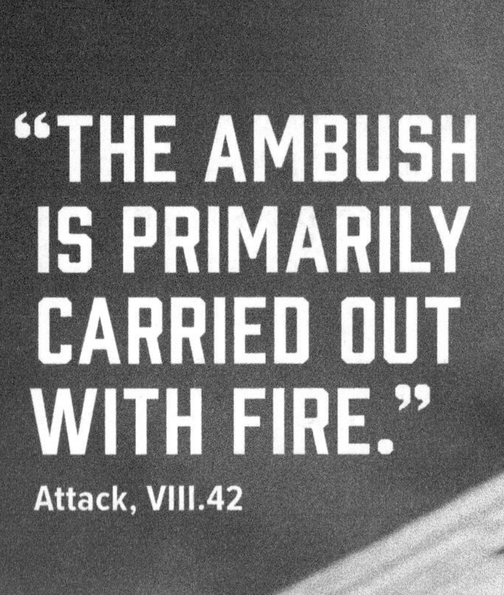
"THE AMBUSH IS PRIMARILY CARRIED OUT WITH FIRE."
Attack, VIII.42

# IX. DEFENSE

**1.** The defense takes advantage of favorable terrain and orderly combat preparation in order to maximize the effectiveness of its own long-range means of combat and to make the enemy's approach more difficult. It strives to smash the enemy with fire before it comes to close combat.

**2.** Pure defense does not lead to a real decision. A repelled attack is only a partial success; it can be repeated by the enemy on a new basis and using stronger means. Only in combination with the attack can the defense lead to a full decision.

**3.** The defender is forced to wait for the enemy's actions and must be ready to repel an attack at any location. Only a strong character can endure this moral burden.

**4.** Surprise is not easy for the defender to exploit because his preparations will be noticed by the enemy over time, despite the best camouflage and secrecy.

**5.** The defender must make every effort to compensate for these disadvantages. He must not wait until he is crushed by the enemy, but must from the very beginning seek every means to actively thwart the enemy's measures. By frequently changing his firing positions and his method of fighting, especially after a repelled attack, he must constantly confront the enemy with new situations.

**6.** The choice of a defensive position is determined by

— the effectiveness of one's own weapons,
— the cover against enemy sight and effect,
— the natural obstacles in front of the frontline.

**7.** Effectiveness takes precedence over cover; however, it must be borne in mind that if there is a complete lack of cover, the weapon and thus its effectiveness will soon go down.

**8.** The leader first assesses a position according to its depth and determines on which strip of terrain he wants to let the bulk of his defensive fire take effect. The center of gravity of the defense lies in this strip; its rear limit is determined by the line held by the main forces.

Only after this does the leader calculate the division into sections and their allocation of troops.

**9.** The clearer the terrain, the more the defense is concentrated on individual points, between which there are only gaps covered by fire. For night and fog, these gaps must be monitored by strong mobile units or by inserting intermediate detachments from the reserve.

Behind the main fire barrier, further fire barriers prevent the advance of an enemy who has broken through.

**10.** Each base is under unified command; it covers its neighbors with its fire. Anyone who wants to cover himself with weapons set up in neighboring sections betrays distrust in his comrades, leaves those weapons to themselves, and exposes them to rapid enemy attack.

At section boundaries, the superior leader orders the cooperation of the neighboring bases.

**11.** In mountainous terrain and behind large obstacles, the defender can limit himself to setting up independent bases that are defendable in any direction at the most important points of passage. In intermediate terrain, mobile forces fight the invading enemy by attack and ambush. This type of defense can also be used if the resources for the front to be held are too scarce; in good terrain, however, it does not lead to success in the long run against superior opponents.

**12.** Additional weapons and troops can be advanced ahead of the line held by the main forces; behind it, reserves are needed in a depth structure.

**13.** Advanced forces gain a certain amount of time, but sooner or later they will be destroyed by the enemy, or they must be withdrawn before they can become sufficiently effective; their loss is to be expected in any case. The leader must therefore decide whether the advantage to be gained is justified by the situation and is worth the loss of valuable fighters and weapons. Weak units that are far ahead and cannot be supported by effective fire from the position are worthless and will quickly go down unless they are highly mobile and favored by unclear terrain.

**14.** No defense of any duration is possible without strong reserves.

**15.** Defensive fire, in its strict sense, is provided exclusively by infantry weapons. Artillery cannot block terrain; it is an additional means in the hands of the superior leader.

**16.** In addition to the weapons whose task it is to smash the enemy with their fire immediately before the front, others may be intended to delay the enemy's movements at a greater distance or to combat his supporting weapons. The quantitative ratio of the weapons to be used for these two tasks is determined by the situation and mission.

**17.** Short firing distances are required for fire intended to bring the enemy to a definitive halt.

**18.** The organization and conduct of the battle are essentially determined by whether the defense is of long duration or a temporary, short-term hold.

**19.** If a position has to be held for a long time or permanently, a sharp concentration of resources in the center of gravity and extensive restraint of fire are required; the leader risks the decision and uses the bulk of his fire only when the enemy has approached to a distance that allows for a devastating effect of the defensive weapons. The bulk of forces is used for defensive fire in a narrower sense. The time gain that can be achieved by advanced forces and early fire is generally not worthwhile.

**20.** If the defensive task is of limited duration, the leader will try to evade the decision and keep the enemy at bay until the assigned time has passed. All measures that promise to gain time are appropriate: long-distance fire, advanced detachments; the majority of long-range weapons use their maximum effective firing ranges.

The stronger the force, the longer it can fight in this way with a chance of success; however, it must be borne in mind that long-range fire is impossible at night; in poor visibility conditions and in confusing terrain, the only way to gain time in this struggle is to fight the enemy with highly mobile and aggressive detachments sent far ahead.

**21.** The planned fire organization must not lead to inflexibility. Any weapon must be prepared to fire in a direction other than that previously determined if conditions require it.

**22.** The leader must take advantage of the easy maneuverability of the artillery fire; the batteries must be positioned so far back that they can cover a sufficiently wide area within their pivoting range. This arrangement and a well-developed network of communications make it possible to prepare concentrated fire from powerful artillery assemblies at important points. Setting up large fire concentrations requires a certain amount of time; the leader must order them with foresight if they are to be unleashed at the right moment.

**23.** The maximum effect of the artillery is achieved by smashing strong enemy assemblies shortly before the beginning of their attack; the leader makes every effort to recognize such positions in good time. If this is not possible, or if the fire has not been sufficient, the artillery works in the rear of the advancing troops and cuts off the foremost attack units from their reserves. Airplanes are used in the same way as artillery.

**24.** Even the best-organized defensive position is not protected against breaches or even breakthroughs by the enemy.

The moment of the enemy breaking into the position is favorable to a determined and cold-blooded defender. The enemy's long-range weapons must cease fire, and man-to-man combat begins. Anyone capable of fighting who does not have an important long-range fire assignment rushes at the enemy and destroys him.

**25.** The more shock troops and other smaller reserves that have managed to evade the enemy's effective long-range fire lie in wait, and the more swift and decisive their reaction, the more certain they can be of success. At this point, surprise works fully in favor of the defender, who attacks the enemy, weakened by losses and exhausted by the approach, at the moment when he feels certain of victory.

**26.** If a breach is nevertheless successful, the leader deploys his reserves to counterattack. To this end, it is crucial that the troops on both sides of the breach hold their positions and seal them off against the enemy, even if they have been bypassed. They form the flanking for the counterattack, which is intended to retake the lost ground. If they run off, however, the entire position will crumble in a short time, and a gap will be created that cannot be closed anymore.

**27.** A counterattack requires arrangements. However, if so much time is lost by this that the enemy can establish and organize himself in the conquered position, the prospect of success is slim.

The leader must sense early on, from the course of battle, where the enemy will make his main thrust and move his reserves close to the anticipated deployment area. The development of the battle situation then allows the location and task to be determined more precisely in various steps, so that the counterattack can be launched within the shortest possible time after the enemy's successful breakthrough.

**28.** Counterattacks are most successful when they take the enemy by surprise while he is advancing further and bringing up his long-range means of combat, hitting him in the flank and at short range. Cutting off enemy detachments that have advanced far ahead is particularly rewarding.

**29.** When recapturing smaller positions, it may be advantageous to wait until dawn or nightfall. If the counterattack has to cross a long distance covered by enemy fire before reaching the enemy, it is often necessary to do so at dawn.

**30.** The decision not to retake important positions but to build up a new front with the reserves behind it is very serious for a defense planned for the long term; the new front is naturally weaker and less well-prepared. Only extreme distress may cause the leader to decide to do so. In the case of defensive fronts that have only emerged in the course of battle and have a haphazard character, the leader would do better to abandon bad fronts without regard to prestige and move the defense to more suitable terrain before the enemy attack begins.

# X. EXPLOITATION OF SUCCESS

**1.** Only the exploitation of a success makes the decision definite.

**2.** The defeated enemy must first be so worn down or crushed with fire from all available weapons that he can no longer come to his senses and has no opportunity to mount an orderly defense. A trapped enemy is pushed together in such a way that he loses all maneuverability, and his formations hinder each other in combat.

**3.** Against a retreating enemy, all available troops, especially fast units, must be used for pursuit, regardless of exhaustion and marching losses.

Frontal pursuit usually does not help much and soon encounters enemy rearguards; instead, efforts must be made to overtake the enemy laterally and to engage him from the flank or rear. Cutting off the retreat at a natural obstacle or bottleneck promises the most success.

**4.** The defender is often not in a position to exploit a defensive success through pursuit. He makes do with pursuit fire and small, mostly nocturnal operations against the enemy, unless a counterattack from the position promises success.

# XI. RETREAT

**1.** A retreat ordered by high command in consideration of the general situation without immediate strong pressure from the enemy at the front must be prepared and carried out with the utmost orderliness. In addition to sending back all expendable units and supplies at an early stage, it is important to build up sufficient protection against the enemy's pursuit.

For this purpose, available detachments are sent back to appropriate sections at an early stage, where they set up barriers at the communications or prepare to flank them or, if necessary, to attack them. It is particularly critical to block parallel roads running alongside the retreat routes. The retreat of the front troops can only begin once these positions have been taken up.

**2.** The front troops fall back abruptly along the entire front and gather on the return roads. Medium and higher formations only gather behind the reception positions; before that, everything remains on the move. If you wait a long time for detachments that have been scattered or are far behind, you run the risk of not being able to evade the enemy.

This type of retreat usually takes place during the night.

**3.** Partial forces must be left with the enemy to simulate the outer edge of the previous position for a short time in order to enable the front troops to march back behind the reception positions.

**4.** Where the task makes a retreat after a certain period of time foreseeable from the outset, the corresponding preparations must also be made in good time so that they can be triggered immediately. Precise reconnaissance and determination of the return march routes are particularly important.

**5.** The rearguards left behind in the reception positions conduct a defensive battle of limited duration. They must be provided with ample means of long-range combat.

**6.** All passive defenses that can delay the enemy's advance are used extensively.

**7.** If the retreat is forced by the immediate tactical success of the enemy, the leader will endeavor to make it as orderly as circumstances permit. The troops that are closest to the enemy hold out to the end and must sacrifice themselves. They are supported by strong long-range weapons, which may also be sacrificed. If there are no more reserves available, the reception positions will be formed by the first units to fall back.

**8.** If it is not possible to wait until nightfall before retreating, the bulk of troops will fall back, making extensive use of the road network and tracks that are less exposed to ground and air sight.

**9.** Retreat battles to gain time can only be carried out by troops with fast means of transportation. In the mountains, this task can also be assigned to infantry that forces the enemy to take time-consuming detours and evades him in good time.

# XII. GUERILLA WARFARE

**1.** Guerilla warfare does not bring about a decision, but it can contribute significantly to it. It has a lasting effect on the morale of the enemy, severely disrupts his command and the supply of his troops, and forces him to take cumbersome precautions and to disperse his forces.

**2.** Guerilla warfare only produces a valuable result if supreme command leads it. Haphazard action by isolated irregulars or small detachments is usually of little use.

Guerilla warfare detachments are not available for the decisive battle and risk being destroyed sooner or later. If you cannot devote a lot of resources to this, it is better to send them from the front on a case-by-case basis with a precisely defined task and for a limited period of time. Command alone is in a position to see where their deployment is most valuable and most necessary.

**3.** In guerilla warfare, neither the number of detachments nor their strength is decisive; only the courage, cunning, and physical fitness of the leaders and fellow fighters are important.

**4.** Guerilla warfare detachments require ample equipment with close combat and explosive means, as well as rations. Hidden camps in the terrain can serve as bases for a longer period of time, and the connection to reliable elements in the population can greatly facilitate the work.

**5.** The activity of the guerilla warfare detachments consists of ambushes and acts of sabotage. The most productive are ambushes on higher leaders, command staff, and other leadership institutions. Night ambushes on troop shelters and bivouacs can cause great panic, in which the enemy inflicts the greatest losses on itself and entire units are incapacitated for long periods of time.

Vehicle columns, especially those with horses, also provide favorable targets. Damaging enemy supplies is only of value where the available supply lines are limited; in terrain rich in communications, it has no lasting success.

Destruction of resources and sabotage of communications are useful if very valuable material that is difficult to replace or particularly dangerous for one's own troops can be destroyed, or if vital enemy lines can be disrupted for a longer period of time.

**6.** The guerilla warfare detachments choose unclear, heavily covered, or mountainous terrain as their field of activity. Only maximum mobility protects them from premature destruction. They usually carry out their ambushes at night; during the day, they can only do so successfully from points that are difficult to access.

An ambush by a guerilla warfare detachment is a short, hard blow that lasts only a few minutes; immediately afterward, the detachment must disappear without a trace.

Repeated attacks on the same enemy unit from different points have a particularly sustained effect.

# XIII. CLOSING REMARKS

**1.** Only those who penetrate into the essence of warfare are able to influence its course; those who cling to its external manifestations are dominated by it.

**2.** Whoever does not know how to distinguish the fundamental from the merely temporal will always remain an amateur.

**3.** An ignorant swashbuckler beats one who is so clever that he becomes timid; lasting success, however, will only come to those who combine willpower with cleverness and cool reasoning.

# APPENDIX

## WHAT IS TACTICS?
## FURTHER READING

3

# WHAT IS TACTICS?

## BY CHRISTIAN VÄTH

### IN MODERN VERNACULAR, THE TERM "TACTICAL" IS USED EXCESSIVELY AND HAS BECOME COMPLETELY WATERED DOWN.

From top to toe, every item of clothing has become "tactical." In its military sense, however, the term has been firmly established since the 19th century and refers to the art of leading a unit on the battlefield. It is not a collection of laws or formulas that can be memorized. There are no recipes for successful combat. Even if the technical means of war are determined by science, it is (so far) ultimately human imagination that determines their use. The practical application of tactics is therefore always determined by a multitude of factors that the participants are often completely unaware of at the time. In the past, particularly capable commanders always had a certain talent, which usually consisted of being able to foresee the course of battle in a high degree of detail before it took place. If these thought patterns are disorganized or no longer correspond to the possibilities of the resources deployed because they are outdated, poor decisions are more likely to be made. However, this does not always have to mean failure. In some circumstances, a tactically well-trained unit can compensate for a commander's shortcomings. Conversely, a good commander can also successfully deploy a force with considerable deficits. Tactics are therefore always linked to decisions, behavior on the battlefield, and previous training.

Tactical thinking is therefore the basis for the decisions that every military leader makes on the battlefield. It is a constant weighing of the advantages and disadvantages of courses of action. The nature of the terrain and the range and effect of weapon systems must be taken into account, as must the supply situation regarding rations and important operating materials. The correct assessment of the enemy's future behavior is particularly difficult. The tactician must therefore always gather and process a large amount of information and then make the right decision. This is never black or white, because tactics are not binary. There are almost always several right and several wrong decisions that can be made. If critical information is missing or there are false reports, even fundamentally good leaders can make the wrong decision. All these processes sometimes take place at breakneck speed, while events come thick and fast. In order to maintain the necessary cool in this chaos, considerable mental strength is required, which can only be achieved through intensive practice. The reliable implementation of a tactical decision by the troops then, in turn, requires disciplined units. In addition to good leaders and instructors, this requires—above all—time and resources. The best decision is worth nothing if there is no one to implement it. Units that are ready for war can adapt quickly to new circumstances and are not only spatially mobile but also flexible in their thinking. They can implement the decision with improvised means as well. Soldiers who think and act independently in accordance with their leader are almost always superior to obtuse underlings.

This type of tactic is called mission-type tactics. While the principles of command and obedience can be taught quickly, training for independence takes a long time. Many people need much longer than the statutory 18 years to reach the age of maturity. Training a flexible, self-reliant, and coordinated force is therefore a very demanding task. Those who pursue this goal only half-heartedly are doomed to failure. The best troops, on the other hand, are worth nothing if no or predominantly poor decisions are made. An army whose commanders are trained to be administrators instead of leaders, and whose units are denied the time and resources for thorough training, is more likely to fail in war. This reality will eventually catch up with those who refuse to accept it.

Within tactics, there are certain general principles that may never change. These include the law of surprise: If you act contrary to the enemy's expectations, you increase your chances, but may still fail. The operational principles of certain branches of the armed forces and types of units do change, but usually at longer-term intervals and more gradually than abruptly. However, technological progress and new ideas for the use of the resulting weapon systems can quickly influence the course of future battles. If these developments are ignored out of arrogance or not noticed due to carelessness, there can be a rude awakening in the event of war. In the short term, tactics can influence the operational or even the strategic level through particular successes and innovations. It is extremely difficult to learn from wars, as they always involve specific contexts that may be completely different from your own situation in the future. It is not enough to copy tactics that have worked for others. You have to develop your own concepts and establish them consistently with the participation of all those involved.

A tactical principle can also define an entire system culture or influence political processes. One example of this is the United States Marine Corps, with its motto “Every man a rifleman.” The USMC has consistently yielded outstanding leaders for many generations because commanders are less likely to lose touch with the most basic tasks of the individual Marine. This, in turn, can mean disadvantages in other areas. The extreme focus on tactical matters can thus lead to a neglection of strategic thinking (example: Germany in World War II). In recent decades, tactics have become less and less important in many Western armed forces, and the training units have become smaller and smaller. In Eastern Europe, divisions are now needed at the front again. The commander of a current division began his training as a tactician in the 1980s. Do his tactical skills still play a role in filling such critical posts? Or are other factors more significant? All armed forces must constantly ask themselves the question: Is our training currently producing good tacticians?

The good news is that tactics can be learned. Once certain basics and knowledge of processes and weapon systems are in place, the so-called war game is a very efficient means of training tacticians, in addition to real exercises with the troops. In 2024, this form of training with Prussian origins will be 200 years old and more relevant than ever. NATO currently has its own initiative to bring these simulations, also known as "serious games," into widespread use.

But as in all arts, groundbreaking works are not created overnight. Unlike weapons systems and ammunition, they cannot simply be bought. Tactics is also much less suitable for political display than a tank. In a society in which fewer and fewer people want to take responsibility for their actions, is the tactician a dying breed? Perhaps artificial intelligence will take over decision-making on the battlefield in the future. At least in this transitional phase that is currently taking place, tacticians will not be able to get by without a solid, analog basis. With relevant principles and the support of modern technology, an experienced military leader can now make the right decisions much faster than ever before.

## CHRISTIAN VÄTH,

*born in 1989, has been an infantry officer (2008–2021) and reserve staff officer since the end of his service. As a freelance lecturer, he conducts basic seminars in strategy and tactics as well as war games for companies and authorities. He is the founder of "Light Infantry International," a training platform for infantry-specific tactics courses.*

**lightinfantry.com**
**lehrmanufaktur.com**

# FURTHER READING

## EXTREME OWNERSHIP

Combat teaches the toughest leadership lessons. Jocko Willink and Leif Babin learned this reality firsthand on the most violent and dangerous battlefield in Iraq. As leaders of SEAL Team Three's Task Unit Bruiser, their mission was one many thought impossible: help U.S. forces secure Ramadi. In gripping, firsthand accounts of heroism, tragic loss, and hard-won victories, they learned that leadership—at every level—is the most important factor in whether a team succeeds or fails.

***"Extreme Ownership"***
*by Jocko Willink and Leif Babin*
*St. Martin's Press, New York 2017, 384 pages, $29.99*

---

## SMALL UNIT TACTICS

A richly illustrated handbook on modern infantry tactics at the smallest level. Anyone who wants to know in detail how a squad and a platoon can operate on the modern battlefield in all conceivable situations will want to pick this up. The authors remain anonymous and are active-duty members of the U.S. Special Forces. The collective has also published other volumes in great depth on individual topics.

***"Small Unit Tactics"***
*Matthew Luke Publishing, 2020, 256 pages, $39.99*

---

## LEADERSHIP AND TRAINING FOR THE FIGHT

Former Master Sergeant Paul Howe is best known for his many years in the U.S. Army Delta Force and his role during Operation "Gothic Serpent" in 1993. Since leaving the service, he has become one of the most renowned shooting instructors in the world. This 2011 edition is an expanded version. In addition to his vividly explained leadership and combat experiences, it also contains a detailed section on his training activities.

***"Leadership and Training for the Fight"***
*by Paul Howe*
*Skyhorse Publishing, New York 2011, 464 pages, $14.95*

---

## THE ART OF WAR

One of the oldest complete surviving writings on warfare. Its timeless and, despite their simplicity, sophisticated principles are still valid today.

***"The Art of War"***
*by Sun Tzu*
*Filiquarian Publishing, New York 2006, 68 pages, $7.30*

---

## ON OPERATIONS / ON TACTICS

If Clausewitz's "On War" is too unwieldy for you, pick up "On Operations" and learn how modern military staff duties came about and how they work. The author's theses on the relevance of the operational level are hotly debated. Friedman also provides an exciting contribution to the discussion on tactics. "On Tactics" is the subject of a lot of discussion in the English-speaking world.

***"On Operations. Operational Art and Military Disciplines"***
*by B.A. Friedman*
*Naval Institute Press, Annapolis 2021, 256 pages, $25.95*

***"On Tactics. A Theory of Victory in Battle"***
*by B.A. Friedman*
*Naval Institute Press, Annapolis 2022, 256 pages, $25.95*

---

## THE 33 STRATEGIES OF WAR

All approaches to warfare, from strategy to tactics, coming in one compact paperback. Each stratagem is described in terms of its universal applicability. The brilliantly written lines can be used everywhere, from everyday decisions to battle plans.

***"The 33 Strategies of War"***
*by Robert Greene*
*Penguin Books, New York 2007, 512 pages, $26.00*

---

## THE NCO AS A POCKET-SIZED GENERAL

Mission-type tactics are often cited as the main reason for the German tactical-operational successes in wars from 1866 to 1945. This study examines this German army leadership principle for the first time by comparing theory and practice.

***"Der Unterführer als Feldherr im Taschenformat. Theorie und Praxis der Auftragstaktik im deutschen Heer 1869 bis 1945"***
*by Marco Sigg*
*Schöningh, Paderborn 2014, 514 pages, $64.00*

---

## THE BLITZKRIEG LEGEND

This study explodes many of the myths concerning German blitzkrieg warfare and the planning for the 1940 campaign. The reader quickly learns what mistakes can be made in the use of land and air forces (even today) and how important logistical planning is. Frieser's groundbreaking interpretation of the topic has been the subject of discussion since the German edition first appeared. This English translation is published in cooperation with the Association of the United States Army.

***"The Blitzkrieg Legend"***
*by Karl-Heinz Frieser*
*Naval Institute Press, Annapolis 2013, 536 pages, $41.95*

---

## COMBAT TECHNIQUE

Written by the author of the infamous guerilla warfare manual "Der totale Widerstand" ("Total Resistance"), this excellent series of publications from the 1970s covers the most relevant combat operations and tactics on the battlefield. In five volumes, some of which come in several parts, the manuals explain everything from basic training to armored counterattacks in clear language and with the aid of sketches. Night fighting and urban combat are of particular importance, with separate volumes devoted to each. Only a few copies are still available on second-hand book websites and can reach prices of several hundred dollars. However, a PDF file containing all volumes is available free of charge via the test version of "Scribdr."

***"Gefechtstechnik" series, multiple volumes***
*von Franz Uhle-Wettler*
*by Hans von Dach*
*Schweizer Unteroffiziersverband, Zürich 1974, 643 pages overall (PDF)*

---

# KNOW MORE

## THE INTERNET IS FULL OF TACTICS—FROM CHESS TO SPORTS—AND YOU CAN ALSO FIND ENOUGH INFORMATION REGARDING THE MILITARY TO FAMILIARIZE YOURSELF WITH THEORY AND APPLICATION.

If you are interested in current conflicts, you can find daily analyses on the website of the **Institute for the Study of War**. At the moment, Ukraine dominates, but there is also Syria, Iran, and more.

▶ Understanding War: **understandingwar.org**

If you want more analysis, especially on topics relating to the **War on Terror** grinding on, the "Long War Journal" is a good place to start.

▶ Long War Journal: **longwarjournal.org**

And then there was unconventional warfare: **Small wars everywhere**. The "Small Wars Journal" interprets them.

▶ Small Wars Journal: **smallwarsjournal.com**

About the Author

# HANS FRICK

Born March 8, 1888, in Zurich, died June 13, 1975, in Bougy-Villars; studied history in Zurich and Munich, 1914 PhD, 1911–1929 infantry instruction officer, 1928–1929 commandeered to the Italian army. Career in the General Staff Department: 1930–1938 Chief of the Training Section, 1938–1939 Deputy Chief of Staff of the Front, 1940 Chief of Staff of the Training Group and Commander of the Linth Group, 1941–1944 Commander of the 7th Division, 1945–1953 Chief of Army Training.

In the early 1930s, Frick brought his political convictions—evolution instead of revolution, Christianity instead of materialism, federalism instead of centralism—to the "Confederate Front" founded by his brother. In 1939/40, he advocated for unconditional resistance in case of a German invasion, and in the summer of 1940, he proposed the army's withdrawal into the National Redoubt. Frick loved to debate and vigorously defended his ideas. He wrote numerous essays on the military and military policy issues, besides being in charge of editing various Swiss military service regulations.

**Works**

— Die militärische Bedeutung der Schweiz im europäischen Kräftespiel, 1935
— Brevier der Taktik, 1943
— Grundfragen unserer Landesverteidigung, 1948

*Biography compiled according to the Encyclopedia of Swiss History (hls-dhs-dss.ch)*

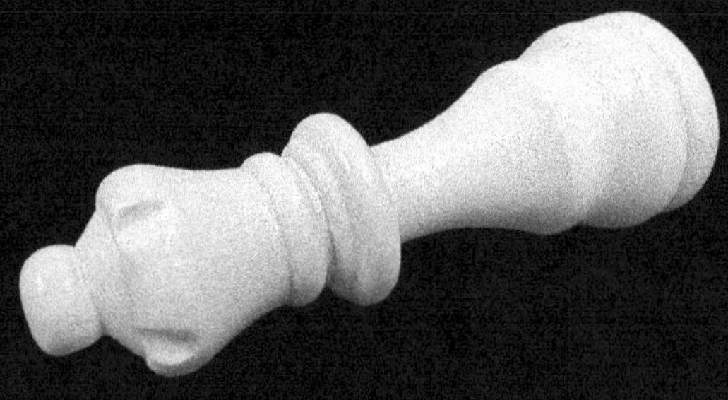

Printed in the USA
CPSIA information can be obtained
at www.ICGtesting.com
CBHW052358031024
15325CB00034B/196